Editor
Eric Migliaccio

Editor in Chief
Karen J. Goldfluss, M.S. Ed.

Creative Director
Sarah M. Smith

Cover Artist
Barb Lorseyedi

Art Coordinator
Renée Mc Elwee

Illustrator
Mark Mason

Imaging
James Edward Grace

Publisher
Mary D. Smith, M.S. Ed.

Author
Heather Wolpert-Gawron

For correlations to Common Core State Standards, see page 8 of this book or visit *http://www.teachercreated.com/standards/*.

Teacher Created Resources
6421 Industry Way
Westminster, CA 92683
www.teachercreated.com
ISBN: 978-1-4206-3824-0
© 2014 Teacher Created Resources
Made in U.S.A.

Table of Contents

Introduction

Reading and comprehending nonfiction or informational text is a challenge. Not everyone can do it well, and it needs to be specifically taught. Students who are great at reading narratives like *Lord of the Rings* or *The Princess Diaries* may still quiver at the possibility of having to understand instructions on uploading an assignment to DropBox. Students who love reading historical fiction may be fearful of reading history. Students who, with flashlight in hand, hide beneath their sheets reading the end of a science-fiction book may glaze over at the sight of an actual factual science article.

Nevertheless, informational text is all around us, and reading it well just takes working out a certain muscle — an informational-text muscle, if you will.

This book is meant to be an informational-muscle gym. Each activity is meant to build in complexity, and each activity is meant to push students in both their reading and their ability to display what they understand about what they read.

In addition to a practice passage, there are 18 reading selections contained in this book. The selections are separated into units, based on their subject matter. As a result, no matter the content area you teach, you will find applicable selections here on which your students can practice.

It doesn't matter what state you teach in, what grade level you teach, or what subject you teach; this book will aid students in understanding more deeply the difficult task of reading informational and nonfiction texts.

Reading Comprehension and the Common Core

The Common Core Standards are here, and with them come a different way to think about reading comprehension. In the past, reading informational text had been compartmentalized, each piece an isolated activity. The Common Core way of thinking is slightly different.

The goal is for students to read different genres and selections of text, pull them together in their heads, and be able to derive a theme or topic that may be shared by them all. In other words, a student may be given three different texts from three different points of view or three different genre standpoints and then have to think about their own thoughts on the subject.

Perhaps a student looks at the following:

1. Instructions on downloading an image from a digital camera
2. A biography about a famous photographer
3. A Google search history on the invention of the camera from the past to the present

Then, from those pieces, the student must pull a common theme or opinion on the topic.

Introduction *(cont.)*

Reading Comprehension and the Common Core *(cont.)*

But to be able to synthesize text (put the thoughts together), a student must first be able to read individual texts and analyze them (pull them apart). That's where this series of books comes in.

Nonfiction Reading Comprehension for the Common Core helps students to hone in on a specific piece of text, identify what's the most important concept in that piece, and answer questions about that specific selection. This will train your students for the bigger challenge that will come later in their schooling: viewing multiple texts and shaking out the meaning of them all.

If you are a public-school teacher, you may be in a state that has adopted the Common Core Standards. Use the selections in this book as individual reading-comprehension activities or pair them with similarly themed selections from other genres to give students a sense of how they will have to pull understanding from the informational, text-heavy world around us.

Copy the individual worksheets as is; or, if you are looking for a more Common Core-aligned format, mimic the Common Core multiple-choice assessments that are coming our way by entering the questions into websites that can help create computer adaptive tests (CATs).

CATs are assessments that allow a student to answer a question, which, depending on whether they answered it correctly or not, leads them to the next question that may be more geared to his or her level. In other words, each student will be taking a differentiated assessment that will end up indicating if a student is capable of answering "Novice" questions up to "Expert" questions.

There are many websites out there that can help you develop assessments to mimic those planned. Create the quiz and embed it into your class webpage or document:

Here are just a couple:

* *http://www.gotoquiz.com/create.html*
* *http://www.quibblo.com/*

Use the selections from this book, and then enter the corresponding questions into the quiz generators. We have identified questions that are higher or lower in level by assigning them a "weight" (from single-weight up through triple-weight). This weight system provides a glimpse of how hard a student should work in order to answer the question correctly. (For more information, read "Leveled Questions" on page 5.)

Regardless of how you choose to use this book, introducing students to the informational world at large is an important way to help them build skills that they will use throughout their schooling and beyond.

Introduction *(cont.)*

Leveled Questions

As you go through this book, you will notice that each question that students will be answering is labeled with icons that look like weights. These icons represent different levels of difficulty. The levels are based on Costa's Levels of Questioning.

The questions in this book are divided into three levels:

Level 1	Level 2	Level 3

These include sentence stems that ask students to . . .	*These include sentence stems that ask students to . . .*	*These include sentence stems that ask students to . . .*
Recite **Define** **Describe** **List**	**Infer** **Compare/Contrast** **Sequence** **Categorize**	**Judge** **Evaluate** **Create** **Hypothesize** **Predict**

The icons are a visual way to make these levels clear to students. That is important because students need to be able to recognize that some questions may require more effort and thought to answer.

Now, most of the multiple-choice questions in this book happen to fall into the Level 1 and Level 2 categories. That is pretty standard for multiple-choice questions. After all, how can asking to create something be defined by an A, B, C, or D answer? However, we may have found a way around that.

At the end of each worksheet is a place for students to develop their own questions about the material they have just read. This brings in a deeper-thinking opportunity. Having your students ask higher-level questions is a great way for assessing their comprehension of what they have read. The deeper the student's question, the deeper his or her understanding of the material.

A student handout called "The Questioning Rubric" is provided on page 6. It serves two purposes:

- It gives your students concrete examples of the elements that make up the different levels of questions.

- It gives you, the teacher, a way to determine whether a student-generated question is a low- or high-level inquiry.

The goal of a student is to ask more challenging questions of oneself. The goal of the teacher is to be able to track better the level of production for each student. This book helps do both.

Introduction *(cont.)*

The Questioning Rubric

Answering questions is one way of proving you understand a reading selection. However, creating your very own questions about the selection might be an even better way. Developing thoughtful, high-level questions can really display your understanding of what you have read, and it also makes other students think about the reading passage in a unique way.

So what types of questions can you ask? There are three levels of questions, and for each one there is a different amount of work your brain must do to answer the question. We've chosen to use a symbol of a weight in order to represent this amount. Consult this chart when thinking about what defines a great question as compared to a so-so one.

Icon	Description
	A single weight represents a **Level 1** question that doesn't require much brainpower to answer correctly. The question only asks readers to tell what they know about the selection. For example, any inquiry that asks for a simple "Yes or No" or "True or False" response is a Level 1 question.
	A double weight represents a **Level 2** question that requires you to use a little more brain sweat. (Ewww!) This question asks readers to think a little beyond the passage. It may require some analysis, inference, or interpretation. Questions involving comparing/contrasting or sequencing often fall here.
	A **Level 3** question really makes you work for its answer. These questions allow you to show off your knowledge of a topic by asking you to create, wonder, judge, evaluate, and/or apply what you know to what you think. These types of questions are much more open-ended than Level 1 or Level 2 questions.

Don't be scared to sweat a little in answering or developing Level 3 questions. Working out your brain in this way will help prepare you for some heavy lifting later on in life. So as you progress through this book, use this rubric as a resource to make sure your questions are as high-level as possible.

Need help getting started? The following sentence stems will give you ideas about how to create questions for each level.

Level 1
- Write the definition of…
- Describe how _____ is…
- List the details that go into…

Level 2
- What can you infer from _____?
- Compare _____ with _____.
- Contrast _____ with _____.
- Write the steps in sequence from _____.
- Place _____ in the right category.

Level 3
- How would you judge the _____?
- How would you evaluate the _____?
- How can you create a _____?
- Hypothesize what would happen if _____.
- What do you predict will happen in _____?

Introduction *(cont.)*

Achievement Graph

As you correct your responses in this book, track how well you improve. Calculate how many answers you got right after each worksheet and mark your progress here based on the number of weights each question was worth. For instance, if you get the first problem correct, and it is worth two weights, then write "2" in the first column. Do this for each column, and add up your total at the end.

Reading Passage	1	2	3	4	Total
"The Five Most Deadly Sharks"					
"Curious About *Curiosity*?"					
"Massive Mountains"					
"Not All Plants Play Nice"					
"What *Didn't* Franklin Do?"					
"Native-American Folklore"					
"The History of a Useful Rose"					
"One of the Amazing Things"					
"Which Holiday Is This?"					
"Finding a Lost City"					
"An Author's Magical Life"					
"A Man with Stars in His Eyes"					
"A Prince on a Mission"					
"Life Among the Chimps"					
"How to Read a Timeline"					
"How to Make a S'more"					
"Creating a Show of Shadows"					
"Which Witch Is Which?"					
"Strange Olympic Sports"					

Common Core State Standards

The lessons and activities included in *Nonfiction Reading Comprehension for the Common Core, Grade 3* meet the following Common Core State Standards. (©Copyright 2010. National Governors Association Center for Best Practices and Council of Chief State School Officers. All right reserved.) For more information about the Common Core State Standards, go to *http://www.corestandards.org/* or visit *http://www.teachercreated.com/standards/*.

Informational Text Standards	
Key Ideas and Details	**Pages**
Standard 1: RI.3.1. Ask and answer questions to demonstrate understanding of a text, referring explicitly to the text as the basis for the answers.	10–47
Craft and Structure	**Pages**
Standard 4: RI.3.4. Determine the meaning of general academic and domain-specific words and phrases in a text relevant to a *grade 3 topic or subject area*	10–47
Integration of Knowledge and Ideas	**Pages**
Standard 7: RI.3.7. Use information gained from illustrations (e.g., maps, photographs) and the words in a text to demonstrate understanding of the text (e.g., where, when, why, and how key events occur).	38
Standard 8: RI.3.8. Describe the logical connection between particular sentences and paragraphs in a text (e.g., comparison, cause/effect, first/second/third in a sequence).	10–47
Range of Reading and Level of Text Complexity	**Pages**
Standard 10: RI.3.10. By the end of the year, read and comprehend informational texts, including history/social studies, science, and technical texts, at the high end of the grades 2–3 text complexity band independently and proficiently.	10–47
Foundational Skills	
Phonics and Word Recognition	**Pages**
Standard 3: RF.3.3. Know and apply grade-level phonics and word-analysis skills in decoding words.	10–47
Fluency	**Pages**
Standard 4: RF.3.4. Read with sufficient accuracy and fluency to support comprehension.	10–47
Language Standards	
Conventions of Standard English	**Pages**
Standard 1: L.3.1. Demonstrate command of the conventions of standard English grammar and usage when writing or speaking.	11–47
Standard 2: L.3.2. Demonstrate command of the conventions of standard English capitalization, punctuation, and spelling when writing.	11–47
Knowledge of Language	**Pages**
Standard 3: L.3.3. Use knowledge of language and its conventions when writing, speaking, reading, or listening.	10–47

Multiple-Choice Test-Taking Tips

Some multiple-choice questions are straightforward and easy. "I know the answer!" your brain yells right away. Some questions, however, stump even the most prepared student. In cases like that, you have to make an educated guess. An educated guess is a guess that uses what you know to help guide your attempt. You don't put your hand over your eyes and pick a random letter! You select it because you've thought about the format of the question, the word choice, the other possible answers, and the language of what's being asked. By making an educated guess, you're increasing your chances of guessing correctly. Whenever you are taking a multiple-choice assessment, you should remember to follow the rules below:

1. Read the directions. It's crucial. You may assume you know what is being asked, but sometimes directions can be tricky when you least expect them to be.

2. Read the questions before you read the passage. Doing this allows you to read the text through a more educated and focused lens. For example, if you know that you will be asked to identify the main idea, you can be on the lookout for that ahead of time.

3. Don't skip a question. Instead, try to make an educated guess. That starts with crossing off the ones you definitely know are not the correct answer. For instance, if you have four possible answers (A, B, C, D) and you can cross off two of them immediately, you've doubled your chances of guessing correctly. If you don't cross off any obvious ones, you would only have a 25% chance of guessing right. However, if you cross off two, you now have a 50% chance!

4. Read carefully for words like *always*, *never*, *not*, *except*, and *every*. Words like these are there to make you stumble. They make the question very specific. Sometimes an answer can be right some of the time, but if a word like *always* or *every* is in the question, the answer must be right *all of the time.*

5. After reading a question, try to come up with the answer first in your head before looking at the possible answers. That way, you will be less likely to bubble or click something you aren't sure about.

6. In questions with an "All of the Above" answer, think of it this way: if you can identify at least two that are correct, then "All of the Above" is probably the correct answer.

7. In questions with a "None of the Above" answer, think of it this way: if you can identify at least two that are *not* correct, then "None of the Above" is probably the correct answer.

8. Don't keep changing your answer. Unless you are sure you made a mistake, usually the first answer you chose is the right one.

The Five Most Deadly Sharks

fr-I-ten-ing

What is it about sharks that humans find so frightening? Is it the teeth? Perhaps it is the fact that they are rulers of an underwater kingdom that we have yet to conquer? People have long been fascinated and freaked out by these predators of the seas.

fa-sin-ate-ed

For example, many of us imagine that sharks are human-hunting villains of the oceans. Does this terrifying image give an accurate picture of these creatures? It really doesn't. The fact is, there are over 370 species of sharks. Only about a dozen of them could even **pose** a threat to humans.

Let's look at the top five scariest sharks:

5. Sand Tiger Shark

4. Requiem Shark

3. Bull Shark

2. Tiger Shark

1. Great White Shark

It's important to know that over half of all attacks are only from the top three on the list. Of those three, the great white is the most dangerous by far. It accounts for more attacks than the bull shark and tiger shark combined.

So why do sharks attack us? Many scientists believe that most shark attacks are, in fact, accidental. Sharks don't want to hurt people. They really don't want to eat us at all. Maybe we don't taste good. Maybe we're just too much trouble. Generally, scientists believe, sharks get confused. They think we are one of their favorite dinners: the seal.

Answer the following questions about the story "The Five Most Deadly Sharks." The weights show you how hard you will need to work to find each answer.

1. According to the article, how many species of sharks could be dangerous to humans?

Ⓐ 18　　　　　　　　　　　Ⓒ 20

Ⓑ 12　　　　　　　　　　　Ⓓ 25

2. What is the most dangerous shark by far?

Ⓐ the bull shark

Ⓑ the tiger shark

Ⓒ the great white shark

Ⓓ the requiem shark

3. According to the article, what is one of the favorite meals for a shark?

Ⓐ humans　　　　　　　　　Ⓒ other sharks

Ⓑ fish　　　　　　　　　　Ⓓ seals

4. Based on the passage, what can you infer is the meaning of the word *pose*?

Ⓐ present　　　　　　　　　Ⓒ reject

Ⓑ dismiss　　　　　　　　　Ⓓ move

On the lines below, write ~~3 of~~ **your own question based on "The Five Most Deadly Sharks."** ~~Circle the correct picture on the left to show the level of the question you wrote.~~

5. _____

_____

6. _____

_____

7. _____

On a separate piece of paper . . .

①• Write a sentence that includes the word *species*.

②• ~~Sharks have evolved to become very efficient hunters. Create a list of adaptations that you feel make the shark such a successful predator.~~ Make a list of things that make a shark a good hunter.

① Write a paragraph (5-7 sentences) using the list you made about sharks yesterday.

Curious About *Curiosity*?

The date was August 12, 2012. After about eight-and-a-half months of travel, the *Curiosity* rover was trying to land on Mars. *Curiosity* is a robot. It is the size of a car. It was sent to Mars to tell us more about the planet's weather and landscape. It may even be able to tell us if life was ever present on the "Red Planet."

The landing was not simple. There was so much that could go wrong! It took many steps. Each step took a lot of planning. Here is how complex it was to land the *Curiosity* rover on Mars:

1. First, the capsule that carries *Curiosity* begins to land.

2. Next, a parachute opens on the capsule.

3. The back shell then separates from the rover.

4. Rockets go off to slow the landing.

5. A sky crane begins to let the rover down slowly.

6. *Curiosity* touches down on land.

7. The capsule blasts off, leaving *Curiosity* on the surface of Mars.

The landing was a success! President Barak Obama made a call to the scientists who made the landing happen. He said, "You guys are examples of American know-how and ingenuity, and it's really an amazing accomplishment."

Even now, the rover is traveling around Mars. It is rolling along, taking pictures. It is sending images back to us on Earth. This could help us find ways to live on other planets some day. The *Curiosity* landing is a first step towards making science fiction a reality!

Answer the following questions about the story "Curious About *Curiosity*?" The weights show you how hard you will need to work to find each answer.

1. Why might scientists have been nervous when *Curiosity* was landing?

Ⓐ They didn't know if the parachute would open.

Ⓑ They weren't sure the back shell would separate successfully.

Ⓒ They weren't positive the sky crane would work.

Ⓓ all of the above

2. If it took about eight-and-a-half months to get to Mars, and it arrived on August 6, 2012, when could *Curiosity* have taken off from Earth?

Ⓐ November 26, 2012   Ⓒ April 6, 2011

Ⓑ January 6, 2012   Ⓓ November 26, 2011

3. What did the president mean by the word *ingenuity*?

Ⓐ bravery   Ⓒ creativity

Ⓑ curiosity   Ⓓ collaboration

4. What was used to slow down *Curiosity's* speed as it landed?

Ⓐ rockets   Ⓒ a parachute

Ⓑ a crane   Ⓓ All of the above.

On the lines below, write your own question based on "Curious About *Curiosity*?" Circle the correct picture on the left to show the level of the question you wrote.

_____

_____

_____

_____

_____

On a separate piece of paper . . .

- Write a sentence that includes the word *complex*.

- Describe the first pictures you think *Curiosity* took upon landing on the surface of Mars.

Massive Mountains

There are many huge mountains in the world. Some are really tall. Others are really long. Others are very wide. Each is unique. Mountains appear on every continent. Let's look at which mountain ranges are the record breakers.

- **Highest Altitude** — Mt. Everest is in Asia. It is considered the tallest mountain in the world. In reality, it's the highest in altitude. It is the tallest mountain from sea level to its peak. The term "sea level" means at the level the ocean's surface begins. So from the surface of the sea to the top of the mountain, Mt. Everest scores the highest. It is about 29,000 feet above sea level.

- **Tallest Mountain** — If we count the base of the mountain to the peak of the mountain, then the tallest mountain is Mauna Kea. Mauna Kea is an island in the Pacific Ocean. We can say that its base is the ocean floor itself. That makes this mountain about 33,000 feet tall.

- **Longest Mountain Range** — The longest range is not actually found on land. It's found underwater. It's called the mid-ocean ridge. It's over 40,000 miles long!

Earth's mountain ranges form a lot of the character on the surface of our planet. What would our planet look like without them?

Answer the following questions about the story "Massive Mountains." The weights show you how hard you will need to work to find each answer.

1. According to the story, mountains can be found
- Ⓐ in every city.
- Ⓑ in every state.
- Ⓒ in every country.
- Ⓓ on every continent.

2. Where is all of the tallest mountain located?
- Ⓐ in Asia
- Ⓑ underwater
- Ⓒ in the Pacific Ocean
- Ⓓ on Mt. Everest

3. How long is the mid-ocean ridge?
- Ⓐ 40 miles
- Ⓑ 400 miles
- Ⓒ 4,000 miles
- Ⓓ 40,000 miles

4. From the information given in the story, you can infer that the peak of Mauna Kea rises _____ above sea level.
- Ⓐ less than 29,000 feet
- Ⓑ more than 29,000 feet
- Ⓒ about 33,000 feet
- Ⓓ almost 40,000 miles

On the lines below, write your own question based on "Massive Mountains." Circle the correct picture on the left to show the level of the question you wrote.

_____

_____

_____

_____

On a separate piece of paper . . .

- Write a sentence that includes the word *surface*.
- Let's say you are packing for a trip to hike Mt. Everest. You can only take things that you can fit into one backpack. Make a list of the important items that you would need for such a trip.

Not All Plants Play Nice

Plants live almost everywhere on our planet. They live in areas full of the vitamins and minerals they need. They also live in places that do not give them their vitamins. One place like this is called a bog. A bog is a swampy wetland. In a bog, there are not many vitamins. So some plants that live in bogs must get their vitamins from strange places. Some eat animals! They eat anything from bugs to small frogs. In order to be able to eat those things, the plants have adapted. They have changed in order to survive. Most plants get nutrients from the soil. However, carnivorous plants have changed so that their leaves do all the work. Their leaves have changed to form different kinds of traps. These traps help the plants catch their prey.

Some kinds of traps are . . .

1. **Pitfall Traps** – Little pools of liquid form on the leaves of these plants. The insect gets trapped in the pool and can't get out. The liquid also helps digest the bug. Pitcher plants have this kind of trap.

2. **Snap Traps** – These traps look like mouths! The mouths snap shut when they sense a bug inside. Venus flytraps have snap traps.

3. **Suction Traps** – The leaves on these plants are like balloons with little trap doors. Bugs get caught inside, and the door slams shut! Bladderworts use these kinds of traps.

4. **Flypaper Traps** – These traps have a sticky liquid on their leaves or stems that traps bugs so they can't move. Sundews use this kind of trap.

You can go to many botanical gardens to see these traps in action. You can even buy some kinds of carnivorous plants. It's not the same thing as having a pet, but it's the closest you can get in the plant kingdom!

Name: _____   Science Passage #3

Answer the following questions about the story "Not All Plants Play Nice." The weights show you how hard you will need to work to find each answer.

1. Based on the passage, what does the word *carnivorous* mean?
Ⓐ "plant-eater"
Ⓑ "meat-eater"
Ⓒ "absorber of sunlight"
Ⓓ "underwater-dweller"

2. Finish the following sentence: In a pitfall trap, the leaves act almost like a human's
Ⓐ stomach.   Ⓒ heart.
Ⓑ eyes.   Ⓓ liver.

3. How many different kinds of traps are mentioned in this passage?
Ⓐ 1   Ⓒ 3
Ⓑ 2   Ⓓ 4

4. Which kind of plant uses a snap trap?
Ⓐ sundew   Ⓒ pitcher plant
Ⓑ bladderwort   Ⓓ Venus flytrap

On the lines below, write your own question based on "Not All Plants Play Nice." Circle the correct picture on the left to show the level of the question you wrote.

_____

_____

_____

_____

_____

On a separate piece of paper . . .

- Write a sentence that includes the word *carnivorous*.
- Think about the carnivorous plants you have learned about today. Now create your own and label the kind of trap that it has.

What *Didn't* Franklin Do?

Benjamin Franklin was a famous American. He did many things. He was a politician, an author, and a great speaker. He even started our Post Office. He was also a great inventor. In fact, many of his inventions are still in use today!

Here is a list of just some of his inventions and discoveries:

1. **Bifocals** – These are glasses with lenses that have two parts. The upper part helps people see far away. The lower half helps them to read up close.

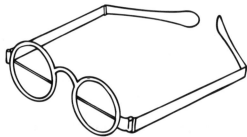

2. **Swim fins** – He made flippers to swim with. They were worn on your hands, not your feet!

3. **Electricity** – Ben did a lot of research on this subject. He helped people learn what it was all about.

4. **The Gulf Stream** – It takes longer to travel west than east across the Atlantic Ocean. No one knew why. Ben finally realized there was what we now know of as the Gulf Stream. He mapped this strong ocean current. This helped travelers.

5. **"Long arm"** – Have you ever wanted something that was hard to reach? Ben made a long stick with a grasping end.

Ben was thinking of new things all the time. Inventing starts with using your imagination. Just think, somewhere there might be a student thinking of other new inventions. Perhaps Ben's success could help inspire other students to make their dreams reality.

Name: _____   Science Passage #4

Answer the following questions about the story "What *Didn't* Franklin Do?" The weights show you how hard you will need to work to find each answer.

1. Based on the title of the passage, the author thinks Benjamin Franklin

(A) was lazy.

(B) was a good politician.

(C) did a lot of things.

(D) invented electricity.

2. According to the passage, Benjamin Franklin invented bifocals. What can you infer the prefix *bi-* means?

(A) cannot see

(B) hard to focus

(C) written by

(D) two

3. Based on what you read about the Gulf Stream, what is a "current"?

(A) a pathway of faster-moving water

(B) something that is up-to-date

(C) a piece of fruit

(D) a ship

4. What makes Benjamin Franklin's swim fins different than the ones we wear today?

(A) They were shorter.

(B) They were longer.

(C) They strapped around the waist.

(D) They were worn on the hands.

On the lines below, write your own question based on "What *Didn't* Franklin Do?" Circle the correct picture on the left to show the level of the question you wrote.

_____

_____

_____

_____

On a separate piece of paper . . .

- Write a sentence that includes the word *invention*.

- Have you ever wanted to invent something? Think about a problem that needs to be solved, and invent an object to solve it.

©Teacher Created Resources   19   *#3824 Nonfiction Reading Comprehension*

Native-American Folklore

North America is full of folklore. A culture's *folklore* includes the stories that its people tell to teach about their traditions. The stories include the beliefs of the people. Folklore is passed down by word of mouth. The older people tell the younger people. When the young people grow up, they tell their children the same stories. Every culture has its own folklore.

Native Americans told folklore. These stories help explain the world. Some stories explain nature. Others explain how Earth was created. For instance, one Cherokee myth tells the story of how Earth was once a floating island. It hung on cords. The sun was on a track that moved from east to west.

Some stories are tales of heroes. Others are tales of "tricksters." Tricksters are characters who taught the listener how not to behave. Many of the stories include lessons. These lessons warn the people about how to behave. The lessons are called morals. The tribes pass down the folklore from father to son and mother to daughter. In this way, everyone can remember the lessons from year to year.

Answer the following questions about the story "Native-American Folklore." The weights show you how hard you will need to work to find each answer.

1. According to the passage, folklore was passed down by "word of mouth." What can you infer is the meaning of this phrase?

   Ⓐ through written words   Ⓒ through people telling stories

   Ⓑ through audio file   Ⓓ through books

2. Which tribe told the story of the floating island?

   Ⓐ North America   Ⓒ the Cherokee

   Ⓑ the Apache   Ⓓ the tricksters

3. According to the passage, what is the opposite of a hero?

   Ⓐ a son   Ⓒ a daughter

   Ⓑ a trickster   Ⓓ a warning

4. According to the Cherokee myth from the passage, the sun "moved on a track from east to west." What is the story trying to explain?

   Ⓐ why we have the tides

   Ⓑ why we have earthquakes

   Ⓒ the creation of the animals

   Ⓓ why the sun rises in the east and sets in the west

On the lines below, write your own question based on "Native-American Folklore." Circle the correct picture on the left to show the level of the question you wrote.

_____

_____

_____

_____

On a separate piece of paper . . .

- Write a sentence that includes the word *folklore*.

- What stories do you know that come from your culture?

The History of a Useful Rose

Can you point to the north? If not, a compass rose can help you. A compass rose isn't a new kind of flower. It is an object that helps sailors navigate. Starting in the 1300s, the compass rose helped sailors find their way across the seas.

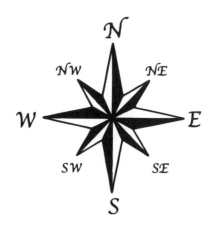

There are 32 points on a compass rose. The points helped travelers find the direction of the winds. Each mark on the compass rose points to a different wind. There are eight major winds shown on a compass rose. These are the South, North, West, East, Southwest, Northwest, Southeast, and Northeast. There are also eight marks that point to winds between those major winds. These are known as the half-winds. The remaining 16 marks point to quarter-winds.

The colors you see the most on a compass rose are black and white. These colors really stand out. Imagine if you were on a dark ship. Even in candlelight, you could see the black marks on the white background.

Now, all charts and maps have some kind of compass rose. The first cartographer to draw a compass rose was Cresques Abraham of Majorca in 1375. The word *cartographer* uses the root word *graph*. That root word means "writing." A cartographer writes maps.

Name: _____

Answer the following questions about the story "The History of a Useful Rose." The weights show you how hard you will need to work to find each answer.

1. How many points on a compass rose are called "major points?"

    Ⓐ 16   Ⓒ 32

    Ⓑ 4   Ⓓ 8

2. In what year did Cresques Abraham first draw a compass rose?

    Ⓐ 1901   Ⓒ 1375

    Ⓑ 1300   Ⓓ 1845

3. Based on what you know about the root word *graph*, what is an autograph?

    Ⓐ self-portrait

    Ⓑ a car

    Ⓒ a self-writing

    Ⓓ a visual used in math

4. Based on the information from the passage, what can you infer is the meaning of *navigate*?

    Ⓐ to listen for

    Ⓑ to find one's way

    Ⓒ to watch

    Ⓓ to lose

On the lines below, write your own question based on "The History of a Useful Rose." Circle the correct picture on the left to show the level of the question you wrote.

_____

_____

_____

_____

On a separate piece of paper . . .

- Write a sentence that includes the word *navigate*.

- Why do you think it is called a "rose"?

One of the Amazing Things

Through imagination, education, and hard work, humans have accomplished so much. An achievement usually begins with an idea. Then people learn how to create that idea. Then they push themselves to finish it. All throughout history, humans have modified, or changed, the world around them to make it better.

One amazing thing that humans build are dams. Beavers also build dams, but they are different. Beavers might build using sticks they find. Humans built using concrete. Dams are built on rivers and waterways. Dams hold back walls of water.

Some human dams help create electricity. They also protect land and homes. Here is how a dam works:

1. A dam holds a lot of water in one place. It keeps the water from flowing like it would naturally.

2. The water in the dam backs up. This creates pressure.

3. This pressure sends water through the intake.

4. The water makes the generator go.

5. The generator helps make things like power lines work.

6. A turbine helps control the power of the water. It helps the water get released back down into the continuing river.

Although beavers may have inspired us, there are no beaver dams out there quite like the ones built by humans!

Answer the following questions about the story "One of the Amazing Things." The weights show you how hard you will need to work to find each answer.

1. What can you infer from the title of the passage?

Ⓐ Humans have only built one amazing thing.

Ⓑ Beavers build amazing things.

Ⓒ Humans have built many amazing things.

Ⓓ It is surprising what humans can do.

2. According to the passage, the word *modified* means

Ⓐ selected.   Ⓒ built.

Ⓑ changed.   Ⓓ destroyed.

3. According to the passage, what moves the water through the dam?

Ⓐ pressure from the water

Ⓑ electricity

Ⓒ the intake

Ⓓ the generator

4. Besides humans, which animals also create dams?

Ⓐ crows   Ⓒ moose

Ⓑ trout   Ⓓ beavers

On the lines below, write your own question based on "One of the Amazing Things." Circle the correct picture on the left to show the level of the question you wrote.

_____

_____

_____

_____

On a separate piece of paper . . .

• Write a sentence that includes the word *modified.*

• If you built a dam, what would you want to have it power? Why?

Which Holiday Is This?

Holidays are days when we celebrate. The United States of America has some of its own holidays. Most people know the meaning of each of these special days. But there are three holidays that get mixed up all the time. They confuse people. The first is Veterans Day. The second is Memorial Day. The third is Labor Day. All three are national holidays in the U.S. Schools are closed. Many workers have the day off. People relax and enjoy their free time. But the three days are not the same. What does each one mean?

Veterans Day is on November 11th each year. It honors people who have served the United States during times of war. The people could be alive or dead. It was declared a national holiday in 1926. This was done by President Calvin Coolidge.

Memorial Day is on the last Monday in May. It honors all of the American soldiers who have died. It began after the Civil War. In the Civil War, the northern part of the country was fighting the southern part of the country. But once this war was over, the U.S. wanted to remember all those who fought.

Labor Day is the first Monday in September. It honors all the workers who have helped to build America. It was named a national holiday in 1894.

So, now you won't have to ask, "Why are we off next Monday?" Now you will know the answer!

Answer the following questions about the story "Which Holiday Is This?" The weights show you how hard you will need to work to find each answer.

1. In what month is Memorial Day celebrated?

(A) May   (C) January

(B) September   (D) April

2. Which president declared Veterans Day a national holiday?

(A) Reagan   (C) Roosevelt

(B) Coolidge   (D) Obama

3. Based on the information in the passage, the word *memorial* might mean

(A) "thinking of soldiers who are alive."

(B) "honoring soldiers who are currently fighting in wars."

(C) "feeling grateful to all Americans."

(D) "remembering soldiers who have died in battle."

4. What were the two sides that fought during the Civil War?

(A) the West and East

(B) the North and South

(C) the Americans and Russians

(D) the French and British

On the lines below, write your own question based on "Which Holiday Is This?" Circle the correct picture on the left to show the level of the question you wrote.

_____

_____

_____

_____

On a separate piece of paper . . .

- Write a sentence that includes the word *honor*.

- If you could designate a holiday, what holiday would you create? Who/what would you honor?

Finding a Lost City

Have you heard of Atlantis? It is often called "the Lost City." This lost city has captured the imagination of many people. Writers have written about it. Artists have painted pictures of what they thought it looked like. Explorers have searched for it.

According to myths, an ancient city sunk into the ocean. The myth says that Poseidon destroyed the city with a huge wave. He was the god of the sea. All of the city's treasures and art sank into the water.

A writer from Ancient Greece first wrote about Atlantis. His name was Plato. He claimed that it sunk 9,000 years before. However, Plato is the only person we know who wrote about this big event. That makes it hard to believe. Wouldn't other writers have written about the story if it were true?

What historians do know is that there once was a real city that was destroyed just like the city in the myth. Its name was Helike. It was off the coast of Greece. It was a leader in shipping. Its people worshipped Poseidon. In 373 BCE, a huge earthquake hit the area. It was followed by a tsunami. A tsunami is a giant wave. The city was destroyed.

Years later, scientists began digging up the ruins of the city. That's when they made an amazing discovery. Helike wasn't the only city to be destroyed in that location! Scientists kept digging. They unearthed different communities that had all shared the same fate. The scientists had a theory. The area was so beautiful and so full of food that humans built cities there. Then, years later, nature would destroy it somehow. Then, another group would discover the beautiful land and build on it. Nature would come back and destroy that next city. In all, six different cities were found in the same area. Each city had been separated by hundreds of years. So they never knew about each other!

Answer the following questions about the story "Finding a Lost City." The weights show you how hard you will need to work to find each answer.

1. Based on the passage, what does the word *unearthed* mean?

  Ⓐ sank   Ⓒ created
  Ⓑ found   Ⓓ broke

2. Think about the pattern of build and destroy, build and destroy. If this pattern continues, what will happen in the area where Helike was discovered?

  Ⓐ Another city will be built there.
  Ⓑ Helike will rise out of the sea.
  Ⓒ Plato will write about Helike.
  Ⓓ Scientists will study Greece.

3. What is the name of the city that really existed and was destroyed?

  Ⓐ Atlantis   Ⓒ Greece
  Ⓑ Poseidon   Ⓓ Helike

4. Based on the passage, what does the phrase "captured the imagination" imply?

  Ⓐ Atlantis trapped people.
  Ⓑ People kept thinking about it.
  Ⓒ Atlantis took people away.
  Ⓓ People forgot all about Atlantis.

On the lines below, write your own question based on "Finding a Lost City." Circle the correct picture on the left to show the level of the question you wrote.

_____

_____

_____

_____

_____

_____

On a separate piece of paper . . .

- Write a sentence that includes the word *legend*.

- Think about an act of nature (a volcano, earthquake, tornado, storm, etc.). Write a myth that tries to explain the event.

An Author's Magical Life

Mary Pope Osborne is the famous author of the *Magic Tree House* book series. This series is about two curious children. Their names are Jack and Annie. One day, Jack and Annie find a magic tree house. The tree house spins them off to far-away lands and other times. They travel to the past and the future. They go on many adventures.

Mary Pope Osborne was born on May 22, 1949. Her father was in the army. This meant that her family moved around the country a lot. At 15, Mary's father retired and her family settled down in one place. Young Mary still craved excitement. She found it in her local theater. There she discovered acting, costumes, sets, and scripts.

In college, Mary found another way to chase adventures: through reading. She read about myths and religion. She read about other cultures and their beliefs. This made her want to travel after college. She went to places like Iraq, India, Crete, and Nepal. While away from home, she read *The Lord of the Rings*. It is a book about a character's journey to far-away lands.

When she got home, Mary Pope Osborne sat down and wrote. She wrote about a young girl who traveled and had adventures. The girl reminded Mary of herself. It began her new career as an author of children's books.

Now Mary has over 45 *Magic Tree House* books in print in 31 countries. She has shared her love of writing and reading with children all over the world. She has also shared her love of seeing new places. As she has said, "Writing is a miracle. You can travel anywhere in the world, to any time and any place — and still be home in time to have dinner."

Answer the following questions about the story "An Author's Magical Life." The weights show you how hard you will need to work to find each answer.

1. According to the passage, at least how many books has Mary Pope Osborne written?

(A) 31

(B) 45

(C) 22

(D) 15

2. When did Mary Pope Osborne first start traveling?

(A) after college

(B) after she published her first children's book

(C) at 15 years old

(D) as a child

3. What inspired Mary to write?

(A) her travels

(B) her father

(C) the military

(D) tree houses

4. What are the names of the main characters in the *Magic Tree House* books?

(A) Jack and Diane

(B) Annie and John

(C) Mary and Osborne

(D) Jack and Annie

On the lines below, write your own question based on "An Author's Magical Life." Circle the correct picture on the left to show the level of the question you wrote.

_____

_____

_____

_____

_____

On a separate piece of paper . . .

• Write a sentence that includes the word *adventure*.

• Where do you think Jack and Annie should go in the next *Magic Tree House* book? Why?

A Man with Stars in His Eyes

Neil deGrasse Tyson was born in New York. When he was nine, he visited the Hayden Planetarium. This is a place where scientists study the stars. Visitors can learn about the stars there, too. This visit showed Neil that he loved everything about the stars. He got a telescope. He viewed the night sky from the roof of his apartment. He took classes about space. He decided to spend his life studying the subject. He went to both Harvard and Columbia. These are great universities. He studied hard to become a great astrophysicist. This is a type of scientist who studies space. Neil is one of the best in the world at this job.

In 1996, he got a job at the same Hayden Planetarium that he went to as a child. Now he is the director there. That is not what Neil is known the most for, though. He is known for how he brings science and space to your TV and computer screens.

Neil has a real talent for taking complex ideas about science and boiling them down so they are easier to understand. He is an author and a TV host. He hosted a show called *Nova* from 2006–2011. In 2013 he began hosting a show called *Cosmos*. He also hosts a podcast called *StarTalk*. He is so good at talking about space that he become an advisor to the U.S. president!

He said, "One of my goals is to bring the universe down to Earth in a way that further excites the audience to want more." He wants to teach people that studying space is important.

Neil is a role model, too. He is one of the only African-American astrophysicists in the country. People listen to what he says. But not all of his decisions were popular. After all, he is one of the astronomers who decided Pluto isn't a planet. Many people didn't like that decision!

Answer the following questions about the story "A Man with Stars in His Eyes." The weights show you how hard you will need to work to find each answer.

1. Based on the information in the passage, what can you guess the prefix *astro-* means?

(A) ocean and water

(B) stars and space

(C) earth and land

(D) clouds and sky

2. When he was nine he visited a planetarium that he also went on to direct when he was older. What was its name?

(A) Hayden Planetarium

(B) Harley Planetarium

(C) Nova Planetarium

(D) Cosmos Planetarium

3. Based on the context of the passage, what does the idiom "boiling them down" mean?

(A) preparing things to be eaten

(B) making things hot

(C) making things simpler

(D) building things up

4. Neil deGrasse Tyson was part of a very unpopular decision that removed Pluto from the list of planets. What does that mean?

(A) People loved the decision.

(B) People questioned the decision.

(C) People disliked the decision.

(D) People cheered the decision.

On the lines below, write your own question based on "A Man with Stars in His Eyes." Circle the correct picture on the left to show the level of the question you wrote.

_____

_____

_____

_____

On a separate piece of paper . . .

- Write a sentence that includes the word *telescope*.

- Look at the list of shows that Neil deGrasse Tyson hosts. If you were writing his next show, what would you call it?

A Prince on a Mission

Prince William Arthur Louis Windsor was born on June 21, 1982. His parents were Prince Charles and Princess Diana. Prince Charles is the heir to the English throne. William was his first child. That means that one day William will most likely inherit the throne. He would then become King of England.

Even a prince must go to school. Prince William went to Eton College. It is one of England's best schools. He loved outdoor sports, like horseback riding and skiing. While at college, Prince William met the girl that was to become his wife. Her name is Kate Middleton. She was not from a royal family. They were married in 2011.

At school, William learned to work hard. It was from his mother, however, that he learned the need to help and serve others.

Princess Diana supported many charities. She taught her sons that they should use their power to help others, too. William and his younger brother, Prince Harry, learned a lot from their mother. After she died, the two boys worked hard to continue helping those in need. William has been to South America and Africa. He helps the sick, the poor, and the young. He helps homeless children. He works to help protect African wildlife.

The whole world watches Prince William. Many remember that day in 1982 when he was born. They have watched him grow up. They are proud of the man that he has become.

Answer the following questions about the story "A Prince on a Mission." The weights show you how hard you will need to work to find each answer.

1. Eventually, Prince William will most likely become

    (A) King of Eton.   (C) King of England.

    (B) Prince of Middleton.   (D) Prince of Eton.

2. How does the passage say Princess Diana influenced her son?

    (A) She helped him learn to spend money wisely.

    (B) She introduced him to Kate Middleton.

    (C) She made sure he knew the importance of helping others.

    (D) She helped him learn to love animals.

3. From what you read in the passage, what does the word *inherit* mean?

    (A) buy   (C) receive

    (B) rent   (D) sell

4. Based on what you read about Prince William, what group might he be likely to help most?

    (A) athletes   (C) doctors

    (B) actors   (D) patients

On the lines below, write your own question based on "A Prince on a Mission." Circle the correct picture on the left to show the level of the question you wrote.

_____

_____

_____

_____

On a separate piece of paper . . .

- Write a sentence that includes the word *charity*.

- How do you think your life as a student now is different than Prince William's was when he was in school?

Life Among the Chimps

Jane Goodall was born on April 3, 1934. She was born in London, England. When she was little, she dreamed of going to Africa. She wanted to learn more about its wildlife. Even as a little girl, Jane would keep a journal of notes and sketches. She would draw pictures of the local wildlife. She watched the birds and animals around her. She read books about animals that lived outside of England, too.

After she grew up, she got a job and traveled to Africa. There, she met a famous scientist named Louis Leakey. Leakey wanted to study chimpanzees in the wild. However, he struggled to find a person who would go into the jungle to help with the study. When he met Jane, he knew he had found the right person. Even though Jane Goodall did not have a college degree or any formal science training, Leakey knew that she was the right person for the job. She was going to live with the chimps and gather information about one of the most intelligent animals on Earth.

To study the chimps, Goodall ate their foods and spent time in the trees. They learned to trust her. She saw that they made tools. They even communicated with different sounds. They made weapons. They even had family groups. She saw the animals comfort each other. She saw them fight each other. She saw them help each other.

Jane Goodall works hard to protect the animals she loves so much. She's written books. She's made movies. She's also created charities. As a result, she has received a number of awards. She was even knighted by Queen Elizabeth. Much of what we know about chimpanzees is because of Jane Goodall. She started out as a young girl who loved animals. She grew up to be a woman who protected them.

Answer the following questions about the story "Life Among the Chimps." The weights show you how hard you will need to work to find each answer.

1. In the first paragraph of the passage, what does the word *local* mean?

Ⓐ nearby   Ⓒ far away

Ⓑ award-winning   Ⓓ busy

2. What is something that Jane Goodall did to get the chimps to trust her?

Ⓐ built a campfire

Ⓑ spent time in trees

Ⓒ set an alarm clock

Ⓓ ate spaghetti

3. What made Jane Goodall perfectly suited to go study chimps in the wild?

Ⓐ She didn't formally study science.

Ⓑ She liked to travel.

Ⓒ She had won many awards.

Ⓓ She loved animals.

4. Who knighted Jane Goodall?

Ⓐ Prince Albert   Ⓒ Queen Elizabeth

Ⓑ King Henry   Ⓓ Louis Leakey

On the lines below, write your own question based on "Life Among the Chimps." Circle the correct picture on the left to show the level of the question you wrote.

_____

_____

_____

_____

On a separate piece of paper . . .

• Write a sentence that includes the word *protect*.

• If you could choose an animal to protect, what would it be, and why?

How to Read a Timeline

A timeline is a graph that shows what has happened over a period of time. For example, a timeline can show you what 100 years in America might look like. It could also show you the events scheduled for one day.

There are different kinds of timelines. Some are rays. Rays start with a mark, like a period. The period represents a moment in time. A ray ends with the symbol of an arrow. That means that time goes off beyond the length of the line. If the timeline is in the form of a straight line with two arrows at the end, then that means that it is showing you a section of time.

The example below shows some important events. All of them took place in America between 1800 and 1900. Each mark represents a decade.

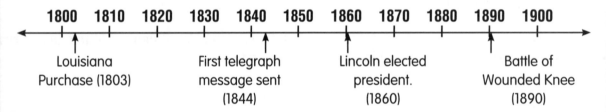

| 1800 | 1810 | 1820 | 1830 | 1840 | 1850 | 1860 | 1870 | 1880 | 1890 | 1900 |

Louisiana Purchase (1803)

First telegraph message sent (1844)

Lincoln elected president. (1860)

Battle of Wounded Knee (1890)

A timeline doesn't have to go across. It doesn't have to be horizontal. It can go up and down. This vertical timeline represents a single school year.

August	—	school (3rd grade) starts
September	—	Jacob comes over to play.
October	—	I make my ninja costume.
November	—	I have a solo in the school Thanksgiving play.
December	—	vacation in Arizona
January	—	I got an A on my essay!
February	—	Caroline gave me a valentine!
March	—	My birthday party was awesome.
April	—	Max comes over to play.
May	—	Spring concert goes well.
June	—	School is out and camp begins!

Answer the following questions about the story "How to Read a Timeline." The weights show you how hard you will need to work to find each answer.

1. Based on the passage, what does the word *vertical* mean?

A up and down

B through

C around

D across

2. What kind of timeline begins with a starting mark?

A a rod   C a line

B a ray   D a pole

3. Based on the passage, which of these time periods is a decade?

A 1900–2000   C 1010–1019

B 2010–2100   D 1800–1803

4. Looking at the 3rd-grader's timeline, which event took place between March and May?

A The student went on vacation.

B The student was a ninja at Halloween.

C The student's friend came over to play.

D The student received a valentine.

On the lines below, write your own question based on "How to Read a Timeline." Circle the correct picture on the left to show the level of the question you wrote.

_____

_____

_____

_____

_____

===

On a separate piece of paper . . .

- Write a sentence that includes the word *vertical.*

- What would your 3rd-grade timeline look like?

How to Make a S'more

Have you ever made a s'more? A s'more is a delicious treat that you can make even while camping. The first known recipe for a s'more was in a Girl Scouts handbook in 1927. The name comes from a combination of the words *some* and *more*. Mash those two words together and you get *s'more*! Once you taste a s'more, you will definitely want some more!

The ingredients to make this tasty treat are simple. All you need are graham crackers, chocolate, and marshmallows. You can make a s'more in just a few easy steps:

1. Find a safe campfire or fireplace. (Make sure an adult is with you.)

2. Take out a graham cracker and break it in half.

3. Select a square of chocolate and place it on one of the graham cracker pieces.

4. Set the "sandwich" aside.

5. Take out a marshmallow and slide it onto a stick with the help from an adult.

6. Hold out the stick to allow the fire to roast the marshmallow.

7. Slide the roasted marshmallow off the stick and place it on top of the chocolate piece.

8. Put the other half of the graham cracker on top of the stack.

9. Enjoy!

Answer the following questions about the story "How to Make a S'more." The weights show you how hard you will need to work to find each answer.

1. What can you infer the word *roast* means?

    Ⓐ cook   Ⓒ chop up

    Ⓑ open   Ⓓ spread

2. According to the passage, what tool do you use to roast the marshmallow?

    Ⓐ fork   Ⓒ graham cracker

    Ⓑ knife   Ⓓ stick

3. What is the author's opinion of a s'more?

    Ⓐ The author dislikes s'mores.

    Ⓑ The author prefers cakes.

    Ⓒ The author loves s'mores.

    Ⓓ The author likes scouting.

4. What ingredients are in a s'more?

    Ⓐ marshmallows, chocolate, toast

    Ⓑ chocolate, graham crackers, butter

    Ⓒ graham crackers, marshmallows, chocolate

    Ⓓ chocolate, marshmallows, cake

On the lines below, write your own question based on "How to Make a S'more." Circle the correct picture on the left to show the level of the question you wrote.

_____

_____

_____

_____

On a separate piece of paper . . .

- Write a sentence that includes the word *combination*.

- Can you make up a word that is a combination of two other words?

Creating a Show of Shadows

Turn out the lights. Now, hold your hand up in front of a flashlight. Do you see your shadow on the wall? Try to make your hands look like a crab claw or a flapping bird. If you succeed, then you have just made a shadow puppet. A shadow puppet uses light and darkness to create pictures for an audience. Unlike most puppets, the audience can't see the object that is making the shadow. A sheet blocks the puppets. The shadow is the only thing the audience sees.

The first known shadow-puppet show was performed during the Han Dynasty in China. It was to entertain the emperor. Even now, over 20 countries have shadow-puppet theaters. It is an art form that is very much alive.

You don't have to be a professional to create a shadow-puppet show. To create one is easy. All you need is a thin screen, a bright light, and your puppet. The puppet can be paper cut out in a shape and taped on a stick. The stick allows the puppeteer to move it around the scene. The sheet hangs in front of the audience. It blocks the puppeteer from view. The light is behind the screen. The puppet casts a shadow on the screen. The shadow moves around like a real performer.

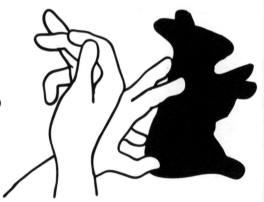

It's really fun to make a shadow-puppet show. It's also great to just be in the audience and watch one.

Answer the following questions about the story "Creating a Show of Shadows." The weights show you how hard you will need to work to find each answer.

1. What are the materials needed to create a shadow-puppet show?

Ⓐ costumes, stick, stage   Ⓒ paper, stick, screen, glue

Ⓑ stick, stage, tape, light   Ⓓ paper, stick, screen, tape, light

2. Based on the passage, where does the screen go in a shadow-puppet show?

Ⓐ between the puppet and the puppeteer

Ⓑ between the audience and the puppet

Ⓒ between the light and the puppet

Ⓓ between the puppeteer and the light

3. As far as we know, where did shadow puppets first come from?

Ⓐ Japan   Ⓒ England

Ⓑ France   Ⓓ China

4. Why do you need the light behind the puppet?

Ⓐ to cast a shadow on the screen

Ⓑ to make sure the puppeteer can see

Ⓒ to make sure the audience can see the puppeteer

Ⓓ to create a heat source for the theater

On the lines below, write your own question based on "Creating a Show of Shadows." Circle the correct picture on the left to show the level of the question you wrote.

_____

_____

_____

_____

_____

_____

On a separate piece of paper . . .

• Write a sentence that includes the word *shadow*.

• Design your own shadow puppet.

Which Witch Is Which?

Look at the title of this reading selection. Notice that the words *which* and *witch* appear in it. These two words are pronounced the same. They sound the same, but they are spelled differently. They also have different meanings. Only one could be used as a costume for Halloween, for example. The words *which* and *witch* are homophones. *Homophones* are words that sound the same but have different definitions.

You can break down the word *homophone* to help you understand it better. *Homo* is a prefix that means "same." *Phone* is a root word that means "sound." Words that contain this root always have something to do with sound.

Here are some other homophones:

- *ant* and *aunt* — "The **ant** is small." "My mom's sister is my **aunt**."

- *aisle* and *I'll* — "She walked down the **aisle**." "**I'll** be there soon!"

- *allowed* and *aloud* — "I was **allowed** to stay up late." "I yelled **aloud** to the baseball player."

- *blue* and *blew* — "The sky is **blue**." "I **blew** a bubble with my gum!"

So how did this happen? Why are there so many words that sound the same but mean different things? It is because many languages have influenced English. Those other languages have given English new words. They have also brought different spellings or definitions to words that are already in English. The end results are homophones.

Answer the following questions about the story "Which Witch Is Which?" The weights show you how hard you will need to work to find each answer.

1. What is a homophone?

   Ⓐ words that are spelled the same but sound different

   Ⓑ words that sound the same but have different definitions

   Ⓒ words that have the same definitions but are spelled differently

   Ⓓ words that are spelled the same but are pronounced differently

2. Which pair of words are *not* examples of homophones?

   Ⓐ *I'll* and *aisle*   Ⓒ *capital* and *capitol*

   Ⓑ *loose* and *lose*   Ⓓ *blue* and *blew*

3. Based on the passage, what does the word *influenced* mean?

   Ⓐ drawn   Ⓒ tickled

   Ⓑ impacted   Ⓓ angered

4. What do the two parts of the word *homophone* mean?

   Ⓐ different-sounding

   Ⓑ similar in appearance

   Ⓒ same-sounding

   Ⓓ similar in pronunciation

On the lines below, write your own question based on "Which Witch Is Which?" Circle the correct picture on the left to show the level of the question you wrote.

_____

_____

_____

_____

On a separate piece of paper . . .

- Write a sentence that includes the word *diverse*.

- Can you think of other homophones? Write as many as you can.

Strange Olympic Sports

The Olympic Games were first held in Greece thousands of years ago. Athletes competed in different events. These Games stopped in 393 CE. After about 1,500 years, a new competition began in 1896. These new Games included many of the sports we are used to watching. There was swimming and running. There was tennis and cycling. But there were also some sports you might not have heard of:

- **Tug-of-War** – A tug-of-war is all about strength. Two teams stand apart. A thick rope is all that comes between them. Each team works together to pull the rope with all of their might. They try to pull the rope toward them. Their goal is to pull the other team off balance. This event lasted from 1900–1920.

- **Swimming Obstacle Course** – A gun sounds. Swimmers race to a finish line. There are obstacles between them and the finish line. They must swim over, under, around, and through different challenges. They have to climb a pole. They have to swim under some boats. They have to crawl over others. This sport appeared only in the 1900 Games.

- **Rope-Climbing** – There are many gymnastic events in the Games. This used to be one of them. Athletes needed to be strong to excel in this sport. They had to climb a tall rope quickly and smoothly. This event lasted for 36 years. It has not been in the Games since 1932.

- **Trampoline** – This event debuted at the 2000 Games. Athletes used a trampoline to jump, bounce, and flip high in the air. To win, they needed to show perfect style and body control. Believe it or not, you can still see this event in today's Games.

Answer the following questions about the story "Strange Olympic Sports." The weights show you how hard you will need to work to find each answer.

1. Of the "strange sports" described, how many are still in the current Olympic Games?

Ⓐ 1   Ⓒ 3

Ⓑ 2   Ⓓ 4

2. Based on the passage, which two events were based on strength?

Ⓐ tug-of-war and swimming obstacle course

Ⓑ swimming obstacle course and trampoline

Ⓒ tug-of-war and trampoline

Ⓓ rope-climbing and tug-of-war

3. Based on the excerpt about the swimming event, what does the word *challenges* mean?

Ⓐ lanes   Ⓒ hoops

Ⓑ obstacles   Ⓓ people

4. Based on the information given, when did rope-climbing first appear in the Olympic Games?

Ⓐ 1896   Ⓒ 1932

Ⓑ 1900   Ⓓ 2000

On the lines below, write your own question based on "Strange Olympic Sports." Circle the correct picture on the left to show the level of the question you wrote.

_____

_____

_____

_____

_____

═══

On a separate piece of paper . . .

- Write a sentence that includes the word *obstacle*.

- What event would you create for the Olympic Games?

═══

Answer Key

Accept appropriate responses for the final three entries on the question-and-answer pages.

The Five Most Deadly Sharks (page 11)
1. B
2. C
3. D
4. A

Curious About *Curiosity*? (page 13)
1. D
2. D
3. C
4. D

Massive Mountains (page 15)
1. D
2. C
3. D
4. A

Not All Plants Play Nice (page 17)
1. B
2. A
3. D
4. D

What *Didn't* Franklin Do? (page 19)
1. C
2. D
3. A
4. D

Native-American Folklore (page 21)
1. C
2. C
3. B
4. D

The History of a Useful Rose (page 23)
1. D
2. C
3. C
4. B

One of the Amazing Things (page 25)
1. C
2. B
3. A
4. D

Which Holiday Is This? (page 27)
1. A
2. B
3. D
4. B

Finding a Lost City (page 29)
1. B
2. A
3. D
4. B

An Author's Magical Life (page 31)
1. B
2. D
3. A
4. D

A Man with Stars in His Eyes (page 33)
1. B
2. A
3. C
4. C

A Prince on a Mission (page 35)
1. C
2. C
3. C
4. D

Life Among the Chimps (page 37)
1. A
2. B
3. D
4. C

How to Read a Timeline (page 39)
1. A
2. B
3. C
4. C

How to Make a S'more (page 41)
1. A
2. D
3. C
4. C

Creating a Show of Shadows (page 43)
1. D
2. B
3. D
4. A

Which Witch Is Which? (page 45)
1. B
2. B
3. B
4. C

Strange Olympic Sports (page 47)
1. A
2. D
3. B
4. A